Lerner SPORTS

GREATEST OF ALL TIME PLAYERS

G.O.A.T. FOOTBALL LINEBACKERS

Alexander Lowe

Lerner Publications ◆ Minneapolis

SPORTS THRILLS MEET RESEARCH SKILLS

Lerner SPORTS

Free Database Trial: lernersports.com

Lerner Publications Company
An imprint of Lerner Publishing Group, Inc.
241 First Avenue North
Minneapolis, MN 55401 USA

For reading levels and more information, look up this title at www.lernerbooks.com.

Main body text set in Aptifer Sans LT Pro.
Typeface provided by Linotype AG.

Library of Congress Cataloging-in-Publication Data
Names: Lowe, Alexander author.
Title: G.O.A.T. football linebackers / Alexander Lowe.
Other titles: Greatest of all time football linebackers
Description: Minneapolis, MN : Lerner Publications , [2023] | Series: Greatest of all time players | Includes bibliographical references and index. | Audience: Ages 7–11 | Audience: Grades 2–3 | Summary: "Linebackers are the leaders of a football team's defense. They lead by example when they lay enormous hits on opposing players. Learn about the toughest, hardest-hitting linebackers in NFL history. Then create your own list!"— Provided by publisher.
Identifiers: LCCN 2021058455 (print) | LCCN 2021058456 (ebook) | ISBN 9781728458038 (library binding) | ISBN 9781728463230 (paperback) | ISBN 9781728461359 (ebook)
Subjects: LCSH: Linebackers (Football)—United States—Biography—Juvenile literature. | Football—Defense—Juvenile literature.
Classification: LCC GV939.A1 L668 2023 (print) | LCC GV939.A1 (ebook) | DDC 796.332/2—dc23/eng/20220104

LC record available at https://lccn.loc.gov/2021058455
LC ebook record available at https://lccn.loc.gov/2021058456

Manufactured in the United States of America
1 – CG – 7/15/22

TABLE OF CONTENTS

THE CAPTAINS OF DEFENSE

In 1986, the Philadelphia Eagles were playing against the New York Giants. The Eagles had the ball on the 5-yard line and were ready to score. Quarterback Ron Jaworski took the ball and dropped back to pass. But before he had a chance to look for open wide receivers, linebacker Lawrence Taylor blasted into him from behind.

FACTS AT A GLANCE

» **LAWRENCE TAYLOR** IS THE ONLY LINEBACKER TO EVER WIN THE MOST VALUABLE PLAYER (MVP) AWARD.

» **JACK LAMBERT** WON FOUR SUPER BOWLS IN SIX YEARS WITH THE PITTSBURGH STEELERS.

» **RAY LEWIS** IS THE ONLY LINEBACKER TO EVER WIN SUPER BOWL MVP AND DEFENSIVE PLAYER OF THE YEAR IN THE SAME SEASON.

» **DERRICK THOMAS** HAS THE NATIONAL FOOTBALL LEAGUE (NFL) RECORD FOR SACKS IN A SINGLE GAME WITH SEVEN.

Taylor tackled Jaworski to the ground. The sack pushed the Eagles back and stopped them in their tracks. The play marked one of four times Lawrence sacked the quarterback that day. For the season, Taylor had 20.5 sacks and won the NFL MVP award.

When a football team's defense is on the field, linebacker is one of the most important positions.

Linebackers are often the captains of the defense. They are in charge of predicting what the other team will do on each play. Then they tell their teammates what to do to stop them.

Ray Lewis retired with the NFL career record for tackles.

Linebackers usually play in the middle of the field. There are two types of linebackers. Middle linebackers play in the center of the field and usually focus on stopping running plays and short passes. Outside linebackers start most plays on the left and the right of the middle linebackers. They might drop back to stop passes, or they can rush in to try to sack the quarterback. The best linebackers can defend passes, stop runs, and attack the quarterback.

DERRICK BROOKS

Derrick Brooks played his entire 14-year career for the Tampa Bay Buccaneers. In his time with the team, he helped to lead one of the most powerful defenses in the NFL. Brooks led Tampa Bay's defense from 1995 to 2008. In 2003, he won the Super Bowl with the Bucs. It was the first NFL championship for Tampa Bay.

Brooks stood out from many other players because of his defense. He had the speed to guard wide receivers and the strength to take on bigger players. His ability to read the quarterback led to 25 career interceptions. He added 24 forced fumbles for a total of 49 career turnovers.

Brooks's biggest honor was winning the 2002 NFL Defensive Player of the Year award. He was also a nine-time All-Pro player and earned a place in 11 Pro Bowls.

DERRICK BROOKS STATS

Tackles	1,713
Forced Fumbles	24
Sacks	13.5
Interceptions	25

WILLIE LANIER

In the 1960s and 1970s, wide receivers did not look forward to playing against the Kansas City Chiefs. They knew that running across the middle of the field would be dangerous because Willie Lanier was there. The Kansas City linebacker tackled any player who dared to go for the ball.

Lanier found a way to break up almost every play in the center of the field. He was the most powerful hitter of his time. But hard-hitting tackles were only part of Lanier's game. He also had great hands and could assist in pass defense. He ended his career with 27 interceptions. That put him far ahead of most other linebackers at the time.

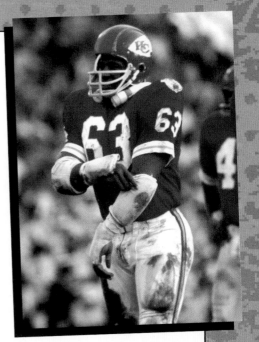

In 1972, Lanier won the NFL Man of the Year award. This award recognizes a player's charity work as well as his performance on the field. Lanier was an eight-time All-Pro and was selected to eight Pro Bowls.

WILLIE LANIER STATS

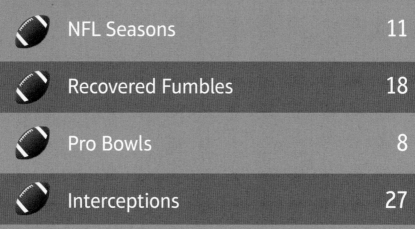

NFL Seasons	11
Recovered Fumbles	18
Pro Bowls	8
Interceptions	27

JUNIOR SEAU

When Junior Seau was on the field, he was always in the right place at the right time to make a good play. This was partly because he was faster than most other linebackers. He was also a smart player who always knew exactly where to go to have the biggest impact.

Most linebackers are good at either stopping the run or defending the passing game. Seau could do both. His ability to be a complete linebacker is a big part of what made him so well-respected during his time in the NFL. He had 10 or more tackles in a game a whopping 64 times in his career. His steady strength made him one of the best of all time.

Seau was an All-Pro nine times, and he was selected to 12 Pro Bowls. In 1994, he was honored as the American Football Conference (AFC) Player of the Year.

JUNIOR SEAU STATS

Tackles	1,847
Forced Fumbles	11
Sacks	56.5
Interceptions	18

A football player's stats might be impressive, but football is a team sport. In the NFL, winning games is the most important stat. No linebacker was more of a winner than Jack Lambert. Fans remember him as one of the toughest players of all time. Lambert helped the Pittsburgh Steelers win many football games in the 1970s and early 1980s.

At his best, he led Pittsburgh's Steel Curtain defense to four Super Bowl wins in just six years. The defense was one of the best in the league, and Lambert was its leader. He was willing to take on the other team's best players to help Pittsburgh win the game.

Lambert was the NFL Defensive Player of the Year twice. He was a nine-time Pro Bowl player and an eight-time All-Pro. He did all of that in just 11 years in the league.

JACK LAMBERT STATS

 All-Pro Selections   8

Fumble Recoveries   17

Sacks   23.5

Interceptions   28

TED HENDRICKS

In the 1970s, opposing quarterbacks had to think twice before throwing passes over the middle. That was the part of the field that Ted Hendricks defended. Hendricks stood 6 feet, 7 inches (2 m) tall.

Hendricks was one of the most successful defensive players in NFL history. He won four Super Bowls with two different teams. His first Super Bowl win came with the Baltimore Colts in 1971. His next three were with the Los Angeles Raiders. Hendricks led defenses with his ability to chase quarterbacks behind the line of scrimmage and stop the passing game. His size and speed made it very difficult for quarterbacks to avoid him when he was closing in.

Hendricks was a nine-time All-Pro player. He was selected to eight Pro Bowls and led his team to seven AFC Championship games during his career.

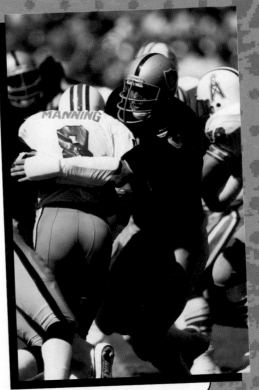

TED HENDRICKS STATS

Blocked Field Goals	25
Safeties	4
Sacks	61
Interceptions	26

DERRICK THOMAS

Derrick Thomas led the Kansas City Chiefs as their sack specialist. He had more sacks than any other player in the NFL during the 1990s. He also set the single-game record for sacks with seven. He retired in 1999 as the all-time Kansas City sack leader.

But Thomas did more than just sack the quarterback. His ability to stop running plays forced opposing teams to avoid the middle of the field. His tough hits led to 45 forced fumbles during his career, an all-time NFL record when he retired.

Thomas was selected to the Pro Bowl in nine of his 11 NFL seasons. Before Thomas joined the Chiefs, the team had made the playoffs only twice in the previous 18 years. With Thomas on the team, they made the playoffs seven times. He was the NFL's most exciting linebacker in the 1990s.

DERRICK THOMAS STATS

🏈	Tackles	641
🏈	Forced Fumbles	45
🏈	Sacks	126.5
🏈	Interceptions	1

MIKE SINGLETARY

The best team defense in NFL history was played by the 1985 Chicago Bears. They allowed only 12.4 points per game. In the playoffs, they allowed only 10 total points in their three wins. The leader of that defense was star linebacker Mike Singletary.

The Bears won the Super Bowl at the end of the 1985 season thanks in large part to Singletary's defense. He was always prepared to play. Singletary was a smart defender who studied his opponents more than some of his coaches did. He could cover people in the passing game, and he delivered powerful tackles behind the line of scrimmage.

Singletary won the NFL Defensive Player of the Year award twice during his career. He was selected to 10 Pro Bowls and was an eight-time All-Pro. His leadership and success on the field make him one of the greatest players of all time.

MIKE SINGLETARY STATS

Tackles	1,488
Passes Defended	51
Sacks	19
Interceptions	7

DICK BUTKUS

The Chicago Bears have always focused on having a strong defense. The team has had many great defenders, and Dick Butkus was the best. He was the most feared man in the NFL from 1965 to 1973 for his ability to deliver punishing hits on ball carriers.

Butkus was one of the first players to force fumbles by stripping the ball. He would grab the ball or poke it out of the hands of ball carriers. No one in the 1960s did that better than Butkus did.

Butkus played for only eight full seasons. Knee injuries caused him to retire early. But he had such a big impact on the position that the award for the NFL's best linebacker is named after him. The Butkus Award recognizes the best high school, college, and pro linebackers. It has been awarded since 1985.

DICK BUTKUS STATS

 NFL Seasons — 9

 Fumbles Recovered — 27

 All-Pro Selections — 6

 Interceptions — 22

RAY LEWIS

Ray Lewis was fierce for his entire 17-year Baltimore Ravens career. In the early 2000s, he was the face of the toughest defense in the league. Ravens fans loved him, and opposing teams were terrified of him. He led Baltimore to two Super Bowl wins.

The best moment of Lewis's career came in the 2001 Super Bowl. The Ravens beat the New York Giants 34–7. Lewis was part of five tackles and defended four passes. He was the seventh defensive player in NFL history to win the Super Bowl MVP award. He also won the Defensive Player of the Year award that season, and again in 2003.

Lewis was named to 12 Pro Bowls, more than any other middle linebacker. He also made eight All-Pro teams. He was the best linebacker in the league for most of his career.

RAY LEWIS STATS

Tackles	2,059
Forced Fumbles	19
Sacks	41.5
Interceptions	31

LAWRENCE TAYLOR

When it comes to the great linebackers of the NFL, no one has ever been better than Lawrence Taylor. During the 1980s, Taylor was the driving force for a series of great New York Giants defenses. Knowing he was on the field changed how opposing teams planned their games.

Taylor's strength led to punishing hits, and he was fast. He rushed past blockers like they were standing still. Before the quarterback knew it, Taylor had another sack. He was willing to take risks that no other players would take. He jumped over blockers or ran right through them. He did whatever it took to get to the football.

Taylor is the only linebacker and just the second defender in NFL history to win league MVP. He also won the Defensive Player of the Year award three times. Taylor's intense play and his incredible skill make him the greatest linebacker of all time.

LAWRENCE TAYLOR STATS

Fumbles Recovered		11
Forced Fumbles		33
Sacks		132.5
Interceptions		9

EVEN MORE G.O.A.T.

Many other great players have played linebacker. Narrowing them down to the 10 greatest of all time is tough. Here are another 10 players who nearly made the G.O.A.T. list.

No. 11	CHUCK BEDNARIK
No. 12	JACK HAM
No. 13	BILL GEORGE
No. 14	BOBBY BELL
No. 15	BRIAN URLACHER
No. 16	RAY NITSCHKE
No. 17	KEVIN GREENE
No. 18	DAVE WILCOX
No. 19	LUKE KUECHLY
No. 20	ANDRE TIPPETT

YOUR G.O.A.T.

It's your turn to make a G.O.A.T. list about linebackers. Start by doing research. Consider the rankings in this book. Then check out the Learn More section. Explore the books and websites to learn more about football players of the past and present.

You can search online for more information about great players too. Check with a librarian, who may have other resources for you. You might even try reaching out to football teams or players to see what they think.

Once you're ready, make your list of the greatest players of all time. Then ask people you know to make G.O.A.T. lists and compare them. Do you have players no one else listed? Are you missing anybody your friends think is important? Talk it over and try to convince them that your list is the G.O.A.T.!

GLOSSARY

All-Pro: one of the best players at their position

American Football Conference (AFC): with the National Football Conference, one of the two groups of teams that make up the NFL

blocker: a football player who gets in the way of defenders

field goal: a score of three points in football made by kicking the ball over the crossbar

fumble: when a football player loses hold of the ball while handling or running with it

interception: a pass caught by the defense

line of scrimmage: an imaginary line that marks the position of the ball at the start of each play Pro Bowl: the NFL's all-star game

sack: to tackle the quarterback behind the line of scrimmage

safety: when a member of the offensive team is tackled behind their own goal line. A safety awards two points to the defensive team.

turnover: losing the ball to the opposing team

wide receiver: a football player whose main job is to catch passes

LEARN MORE

Chicago Bears Linebackers
https://www.si.com/nfl/Best-Chicago-Bears-Linebackers-All-Time

Football
https://kidskonnect.com/sports/football/

Leventhal, Josh. *Linebackers*. Mankato, MN: Black Rabbit Books, 2017.

Levit, Joseph. *Football's G.O.A.T.: Jim Brown, Tom Brady, and More*. Minneapolis: Lerner Publications, 2019.

Linebackers
https://www.ducksters.com/sports/football/linebacker.php

Scheff, Matt. *The Super Bowl: Football's Game of the Year*. Minneapolis: Lerner Publications, 2021.

INDEX

PHOTO ACKNOWLEDGMENTS

Image credits: Icon Sports Media/Newscom, p.4; Rob Tringali/SportsChrome/ Newscom, p.5; Dan Beineke/Stringer/Getty Images, p.6; Michael Zito/ SportsChrome/Newscom, p.7; Al Messerschmidt/Staff/Getty Images, p.8; Scott Halleran/Staff/Getty Images, p.9; David Durochik/Associated Press, p.10; Tony Tomsic/Associated Press, p.11; Icon Sports Media/Newscom, p.12; Donald Miralle/ Staff/Getty Images, p.13; MITCHELL REIBEL/"Ai Wire Photo Service"/Newscom, p.14; SportsChrome/Newscom, p.15; Getty Images/Staff/Getty Images, p.16; George Rose/Stringer/Getty Images, p.17; Cliff Welch/Icon SMI/Newscom, p.18; Tim DeFrisco/Stringer/Getty Images, p.19; SportsChrome/Newscom, p.20; BOB LANGER/Chicago Tribune/Newscom, p.21; TSN/Icon SMI/Newscom, p.22; TSN/Icon SMI/Newscom, 23; Image of Sport/Kirby Lee/Newscom, p.24; Al Bello/Staff/Getty Images, p.25; Al Golub/ZUMA Press/Newscom, p.26; John Barrett/ZUMAPRESS/ Newscom, p.27

Cover: Matt Stroshane/Stringer/Getty Images; Image of Sport/Kirby Lee/ Newscom; Rob Tringali/SportsChrome/Newscom